NORFOLK'S RAILWAY HERITAGE

With aerial photographs by Mike Page

NORFOLK'S RAILWAY HERITAGE

GRAHAM KENWORTHY & RICHARD ADDERSON
PHOTOGRAPHS BY MIKE PAGE

HALSGROVE

First published in Great Britain in 2009

British Library Cataloguing-in-Publication Data
A CIP record for this title is available from the British Library

ISBN 978 1 84114 946 2

HALSGROVE
Halsgrove House,
Ryelands Industrial Estate,
Bagley Road, Wellington, Somerset TA21 9PZ
Tel: 01823 653777   Fax: 01823 216796
email: sales@halsgrove.com

Part of the Halsgrove group of companies
Information on all Halsgrove titles is available at: www.halsgrove.com

Printed and bound in India on behalf of JFDi Print Services Ltd

INTRODUCTION

For some years it has been Mike Page's ambition to produce a book featuring his photographs of Norfolk's railways from the air. Graham Kenworthy and Richard Adderson were delighted to have the opportunity of working with Mike and his fine pictures to help him achieve this aim.

With one exception, all the photographs were taken by Mike Page between 2001 and 2009. The "odd man out" is the black and white image of Hunstanton, and we are most grateful to Slim Wilkinson for allowing us to use this evocative scene. Thanks are also due to Adrian Whittaker for providing the map.

We hope that our selection of pictures, ranging from today's 100 mph electric trains to fading traces of railways abandoned in the 1950s, is wide enough to satisfy the most critical of readers, and we make no apologies for straying briefly over the border into adjacent counties where it was necessary to complete the story. Inevitably, there are several views of one or two places of particular interest, whilst we have been unable to feature other, equally fascinating, locations for the simple reason that all worthwhile traces of the railway have vanished with the passing years.

Each caption has an accompanying symbol, indicating the general direction in which the photograph was taken. For example, ↑ indicates northwards, ↘ indicates south eastwards and ↖ indicates north westwards.

Mike Page, Graham Kenworthy and Richard Adderson

Norfolk Railways

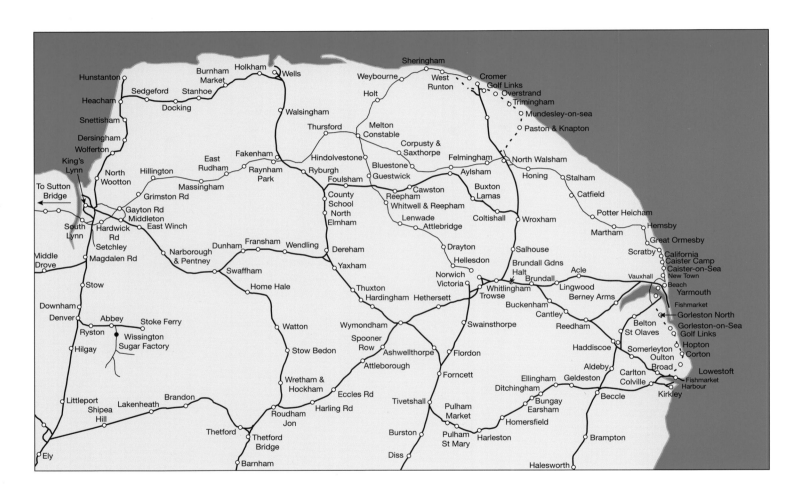

The M&GN – across the county fifty years on.

The lines covered here, which in 1893 became known as the Midland & Great Northern Joint, were an amalgamation of routes opened by a number of different companies between 1864 and 1883. All these lines closed to passengers in February 1959, but some sections were retained for a few years for freight traffic.

Sutton Bridge ⬉

Although located a couple of miles outside the county boundary, Sutton Bridge is, to most people, the western gateway to Norfolk. The Cross Keys swing bridge was shared by road and rail until 1959 with the road on the north side. The station occupied a site off to the left of this view.

Sutton Bridge ↘
The road originally followed a sharp S-bend immediately to the east of the bridge and headed across the narrow embankment to the left of the present, wider road which follows the line of the railway eastwards towards Kings Lynn.

South Lynn ←

Following the alignment of the old railway, the A17 from Sutton Bridge joins the A47 towards the top of the picture before the latter crosses the Great Ouse, heading for the site of the former South Lynn station. The Ely-Kings Lynn line, which the main M&GN route crossed by a bridge, passes from left to right and was joined at Harbour Junction by the spur from South Lynn just out of shot to the right.

Peddars Way ↘

Three miles east of Hillington the A148 road is crossed by Peddars Way, with the former railway route cutting across diagonally from bottom right. During World War II the light coloured, rectangular area served as a rail connected Air Ministry fuel depot; its previous use, during the first decade of the 20th century, was as a source of ballast for the M&GN, a role evidenced by the survival of the semi-circular scooped areas in the field to the south.

Massingham ↖

The single-chimneyed stationmaster's house adjoins the road north of Little Massingham, with the white painted, former station offices further to the east; another original building survives on the opposite platform. Extensions and new houses seem to proliferate, but the extensive gardens towards the signal box add an air of rural tranquillity.

East Rudham ➔

The station buildings, complete with slate roofs and typical barge boards on the gable ends, have received sensitive restoration. The new extension at the north-eastern end is in keeping with the original design; even the awning, which is a recent addition, looks as though it has been there since steam-hauled trains chugged through.

Raynham Park ←

The one feature obviously absent from this location fifty years after closure is the track. Most railway buildings, including the level crossing gate, have survived virtually unaltered; the nearest building and the coach in the platform are the only additions to the site.

Langor Bridge ↖

For the last half-century, this signal box without a railway has been a familiar sight to the east of the A1067 road two miles or so from Fakenham. It was built in 1898 and controlled the level crossing and a siding which saw local coal deliveries and dispatch of locally-grown sugar beet.

Piggs Grave ➜
The railway ran diagonally from bottom left to top right past Gunthorpe gatehouse with its small cabin from which protecting signals were operated. It lies at the highest point on the M&GN system, known as Pigg's Grave summit. The present owner has even retained the identifying gatehouse number 16 on the gable end to the right of the cabin.

Melton Constable ↖

Industrial units, which include several original railway buildings, mask the line through the station. The route to Norwich City describes a gentle arc before heading southwards while the Yarmouth line initially follows a straight course to the south-east. Terraced housing of the railway village in the centre contrasts with the more spacious modern estate to the right.

Melton Constable ←

The industrial, rather than agricultural, nature of this North Norfolk village is encapsulated by the rows of terraced housing provided by the railway company.

Melton Constable ←

The massive water tank at the western end of the site served the whole complex and looks to be in need of a coat of paint. It has the initials M&GN cast into its sides and has recently become the focus of a preservation project.

Felmingham ↑
Situated on a minor road about half a mile south of the village, the station building remains virtually unchanged fifty years after closure. It is seen surrounded by scaffolding, undergoing refurbishment. The former stationmaster's house is now a private residence, while the track, just visible through the trees beyond, leads to a car park on the Weavers Way footpath which follows the railway from North Walsham towards Aylsham.

North Walsham ↖

The M&GN line made its entry to North Walsham along the right-hand edge of the playing field towards the top, underneath the Bittern Line, and along the line of the road towards Honing at the bottom left-hand corner; the route from Mundesley came in from the top right-hand corner. The Bittern Line station and condensate sidings dominate the centre of the picture.

Stalham ↘

The A149 road which bisects this view marks the direction taken by the railway towards Catfield and Potter Heigham. Until the station building was re-erected at Holt on the North Norfolk Railway in 2001/2, both it and the goods yard occupied the partially re-developed site adjacent to the road into the village.

California ↖

After meandering its way through Broadland, the line reached the North Sea in rather dramatic fashion as shown here at California. From a point towards the top-centre of the picture, it made a bee-line for the coast before curving sharply to the south to avoid falling into the water.

Caister on Sea ↖

The curve mentioned in the previous picture can be made out in the distance before the line took refuge behind the dunes as it passed Caister Camp. It then moved slightly further inland, following the line of greenery to Caister station which was located just above the brightly painted lifeboat station.

Caister on Sea ⬇

The lifeboat station in the foreground again helps to pinpoint where we are. After the final short curve to take the route between the eastern side of Yarmouth racecourse and the caravan park, the train would head on a dead straight course to the heart of the resort at Beach station.

Yarmouth ↑
The route into the town followed the eastern side of the racecourse at the top of the picture and then headed due south to Beach station. Much of the formation has been obliterated by buildings but the site of the terminus, on the left of the sports ground at the bottom of the picture, is unmistakable. After fifty years the area remains undeveloped, and provides parking facilities close to the seafront.

Hindolvestone ↑
Having visited the seaside we now return to Melton Constable, which is at the top of the picture. We have already seen the route of the Norwich line branching away, and here it is a little further south, clearly defined as it heads across open fields and through a wooded area towards Hindolvestone.

Hindolvestone ↘

The old station building has been renovated and extended, displaying an abundance of gables and dormer windows. A railway van stands at the former platform providing useful storage.

Guestwick ⬐
A couple of miles further south, this station building also provides nostalgic residential accommodation, but with rather more restrained alterations. The well maintained signal box and retention of the platform wall leaves the observer in no doubt as to the building's former use.

Themelthorpe ⬊

After closure of the M&GN line to passenger traffic, Norwich City Station continued to handle a considerable goods traffic. To shorten the route taken from Norwich Thorpe, a curve was built to join the line which ran east from Wroxham via Reepham to that running south-east to Lenwade. The sharp curve joining what were, at this point, two parallel lines can be seen in the left foreground.

Themelthorpe ⬇

Part of the curve can be seen again in this view, with the M&GN gatehouse nestling in the trees. The former routes now form the Marriott's Way footpath from Aylsham via Reepham and Lenwade to Hellesdon; the path is named after William Marriott, Chief Engineer and Manager of the M&GN for 41 years.

Whitwell ↑

Marriott's Way heads south, well protected by fifty years of tree growth, towards the long-neglected Whitwell & Reepham station. In September 2008 the track panels and coach in the former goods yard are the first signs of a restoration scheme which reached a notable landmark when a steam locomotive operated on the site just five months later.

Lenwade ↘

The first of the rail served industrial units was established prior to passenger closure and continued to generate traffic subsequently. Following complete closure in the early 1980s, the industrial premises have continued to function hemmed in between the Fakenham to Norwich road to the right and the former railway formation to the left.

Norwich City ↖
The railway snaked its way in from Drayton through the north-western part of the city to its terminus on Barn Road adjacent to what is now the roundabout on the inner ring road. A wide expanse of land between Heigham Street and the River Wensum, now covered by retail and light industrial units, indicates the extent and importance of the former railway goods yard.

Ipswich main line – a modern electric railway.
Opening in stages from London, this line linked Norwich with Ipswich and the capital by 1849.
Over the years it gradually assumed a greater importance than the slightly older route via Ely, and by
the 1950s the best trains were taking just two hours for the journey. The line was electrified in 1987.

Thrandeston ↖

About two miles south of Diss station lies an area shown on Ordnance Survey maps as "The Marsh" but known to generations of local railwaymen as "Thrandeston Bog". It is not known how many tons of ballast have disappeared into its depths since the line was opened in 1849 in order to maintain track level. The major work undertaken by Network Rail during 2008 is the first serious attempt to stabilise the whole area – only time will tell if it has been successful.

Diss ←

This is the only intermediate station remaining open in Norfolk on the Ipswich line. Once there were six, the others being at Swainsthorpe, Flordon, Forncett, Tivetshall and Burston. In 2009 the station enjoyed a half-hourly service in each direction for much of the day, and travellers could reach Liverpool Street in less than 100 minutes. Passenger usage has soared in recent years, and the well-occupied car parking spaces reflect the popularity of the train service.

Tivetshall ↖

Until 1953 passengers could change here for the Waveney Valley line across to Beccles. The station itself survived until 1966, and was subsequently demolished. Little trace of it remained in 2008, as a typical London to Norwich train raced over the level crossing, passing the area once occupied by the platforms and station buildings. Above the locomotive, the brick-built goods shed contrasts with the modern structures around it.

Wash Lane, north of Tivetshall ←
Until refurbishment work took place on this minor bridge during electrification work in the mid-1980s one of the coping stones displayed a piece of mid-19th century graffiti. This took the form of the depiction of a rather primitive type of railway locomotive somewhat similar to Stephenson's *Rocket*, that is to say, little more than a boiler on wheels.

Lakenham 🡧
With the site of Norwich Cattle Market in the background, a class 90 electric locomotive propels a train from Liverpool Street over the viaduct spanning the Ely line in February 2008.

Trowse Lower Junction 🡔
Approaching the junction with the Breckland Line, no 70013 "Oliver Cromwell" heads a special train for Norwich along the electrified line from Ipswich. This engine is one of the Britannia class which hauled the crack expresses between Norwich and London during the 1950s. After working the last steam train on British Railways in 1968 it spent some 35 years at Bressingham Museum, before being restored for use on special trains. It made two welcome return trips to what can be regarded as its native county in September 2008.

Norwich ↑

The junction seen in the previous picture is on the bottom right hand side of the picture, and the course of the railway can be followed as it curves round to the north of the football ground and into the station. From this height, we have a unique view of all three of the city's railway termini – or at least the course of the lines leading to them. The original route of the line from Colchester is to the right of the large white building at the bottom centre and cuts through the residential areas of Lakenham, passing under four road bridges as it heads for what was once Norwich Victoria station. This closed to passengers as long ago as 1916, but the line was used by goods trains for another 70 years. The track is now the Lakenham Way footpath, and the sites of the station and goods yard, close to Queens Road and St Stephens, are now occupied by an office block and supermarket respectively. Completing the trio, the curved green strip of Marriott's Way to the north of the city indicates the course of the M&GN line, which we saw more closely on page 29.

Norfolk's little railways.

Whilst Wales is well known for its Great Little Trains, Norfolk can boast
more narrow gauge and miniature lines than most counties.
Here are three of these smaller railways.

Wroxham ⬉

The 15 inch gauge Bure Valley Railway was built on the trackbed of the former branch line between Wroxham and Aylsham, and has become a popular tourist attraction since it opened in 1990. A group of people is standing at the platform end to watch the engine using the turntable at the Wroxham terminus. The tracks of the Bittern Line are in the foreground, and the former main line signalbox is undergoing restoration, prior to being incorporated in the Bure Valley station complex.

West of Coltishall ↗

A footpath and cycleway runs parallel to the railway for its entire length, and this train is passing a couple of walkers as it heads westwards between Coltishall and Buxton. The narrow gauge line and pathway are easily accommodated on the land formerly occupied by the full size railway.

West of Coltishall 🖝
During the summer months there is usually a two-train service over the nine-mile long railway, and trains pass at one of the three passing loops. This meeting is at Little Hautbois, an otherwise quiet spot in the meadows alongside the Bure.

Buxton ↖

A train from Wroxham crosses the River Bure as it approaches Buxton. The bridge has been adapted to carry both the railway and footpath over the river.

Aylsham ⬋

The terminus stands on the site of the old Great Eastern Railway station, all traces of which have vanished in the redevelopment. Even the road bridge which spanned the railway has gone, but the footpath on the far side of the road follows the alignment of the tracks which once continued on towards Reepham and, ultimately, County School.

Aylsham ⬊

Its rails may be only 15 inches apart, but the course of the railway is clearly defined from the air. The station, with its overall roof and extensive car park, is at the bottom of the picture, and the line curves round to tunnel under the Cromer Road before heading out across the fields towards Buxton.

Ashmanhaugh ↗

Not far from the Bure Valley is the Ashmanhaugh Light Railway, a 7¼-inch gauge railway which first ran in 2003. It has been built and is operated by a small group of enthusiasts, and holds public open days during the summer. A train stands at the main station in the middle of the two circuits which form a figure of eight, while the covered carriage shed is at centre bottom. At top left, a further extension is taking shape.

Ashmanhaugh →

By September 2008 the new track was complete, and a lake had been created to provide scenic interest. The path of the tracks is clearly shown from the air, and offers a variety of running options.

Ashmanhaugh ↗
A closer look at the station area shows the signal box which controls operations, while the locos are being prepared for a day's operating. Behind it, the red roofed building provides workshop, clubhouse and refreshment facilities.

Hemsby ↗
Another 7¼-inch gauge line runs through the grounds of a holiday park at this seaside village. Here we can follow the path of the railway as it weaves a sinuous route around the site, with the cars and chalets giving some idea of the scale of the operation.

Hemsby ↑
Parkland Central is the main station on the line, and the complex track layout is fully signalled. Two steam locomotives head trains ready to run round the circuit, although as yet they can boast only three passengers between them. Other locomotives are waiting by the turntable and outside the engine shed to the right of the picture.

The Wherry Lines – following the waterways to the coast.

The "Wherry Lines" tag was first applied in the 1970s. It is used to cover the three local routes from Norwich to the East Coast – to Yarmouth via both Reedham and Acle and to Lowestoft. Two of these lines are amongst the oldest in the area; Norwich – Reedham – Yarmouth dating from 1844 and Reedham – Lowestoft from 1847. Brundall – Acle – Yarmouth was opened somewhat later, in 1883.

Whitlingham ↑

When the railway from Norwich to Yarmouth was built, a new channel for the River Yare was excavated on the south side of the approved route of the line. The original course was via what is now River Green in Thorpe St. Andrew. This arrangement was necessary to maintain access upstream to Norwich for waterborne trade.

Whitlingham ↖

A rather damp day marred the rare visit of a steam hauled train on the Wherry Line. But these weather conditions have their compensation in that the engine's exhaust tends to be more spectacular; this phenomenon is well illustrated here as "Taw Valley" passes the deserted viewpoint of the outside dining area at the Rushcutters pub.

Brundall ↖

A special train with two diesel locomotives "top and tail" passes between the staggered platforms of the station. Station Road level crossing, adjacent to the footbridge, is one of the few traditional gated crossings still operated by a crossing keeper.

Below:

Buckenham ↗

On Summer Saturdays through trains from Liverpool Street to Yarmouth are diesel hauled to their destination without having the electric locomotive removed at Norwich. Here is one such train passing the station on its way to the coast. The building behind the first engine is probably one of the oldest remaining railway buildings in Norfolk, dating from 1844.

Cantley ↗

The appearance of a thirteen-coach train on these lines is a very unusual occurrence. Here is one such rarity passing a Sugar Beet factory settling pond between Cantley and Reedham. Hill Farm, Limpenhoe, appears in the background on the rising ground above the marshes.

Reedham ←

Prominent next to the distant bridge, which carries the road from the Freethorpe direction, are the disused station buildings and the former Stationmaster's house. The station footbridge and platforms can be seen beyond this bridge. On the nearside, the access road through the long abandoned goods yard leads towards the 3-arch bridge which masks Reedham Junction signal box.

Berney Arms ↓

A lonely looking railcar heads away towards Reedham passing the sign which indicates the nearby presence of the station to all who might otherwise miss it. The nearest road is 2 miles to the right while Yarmouth can be reached to the left by following the Weavers Way footpath for 5 miles. Either way, it would appear that stout, waterproof footwear might be required.

Berney Arms ←
The juxtaposition of a main line train, including an electric locomotive, and this extremely remote station is something of a contradiction and is a situation which is rarely photographed. It is possible because of a franchise requirement that National Express provide through trains from Liverpool Street to Yarmouth on a certain number of Summer Saturdays.

Reedham ↗

The 1844 line from Norwich to Yarmouth curves away past the church while the 1847 branch from Reedham to Lowestoft heads towards the River Yare and over the swing bridge. From 1847 until the 1870s there was a line connecting them, so that trains could run directly between the North Sea ports. Well over a century later, the route of this connection is as obvious as ever.

Reedham ↖

The majority of the village, with its extensive river frontage, can be seen in the background as this special train negotiates the sharp curve on the south side of the swing bridge, heading for Lowestoft. There is also a sharp curve on the north side and the line on which the train had approached Reedham can be seen in the top centre of the view.

Reedham 🖝

This bridge replaced the original single track bridge in 1904 when the final section of line between Reedham and Lowestoft was doubled. The original bridge was located a few yards to the left. The yellow strip on the track beneath the 3-car diesel unit is the non-slip walkway, provided for the signalman to reach his signal box.

New Cut ⬋
Hopefully it is the helmsman of the cruiser who may well be saying "Don't look now, but we're being overtaken", as the train accelerates after negotiating Reedham Swing Bridge and the subsequent curve at reduced speed.

New Cut ⬎

The railway alongside the New Cut between Reedham and Haddiscoe has always been susceptible to high tides. The flooding which closed the line in 2007 was the worst since the infamous events of 1953. Considerable damage to the railway was caused by the nearer inundation and machines can be seen replacing the tons of ballast which had been washed into the adjacent fields. Lowestoft can be seen in the distance.

Somerleyton ↑

The idyllic location of the swing bridge linking Norfolk and Suffolk is emphasised in this view of its surroundings. It is of the same design and of a similar date to that already seen at Reedham. A former signalman here has described the pleasure he had watching spectacular sunrises and sunsets, not to mention visits from the local wildlife. No doubt the occupier of the house could tell similar tales.

Somerleyton ↗
Close-up views of the bridge in the open position are only possible to the public from the air or a boat. The operational process involved is a tribute to the early engineers, although modern technology has been introduced where it has been shown to be an advantage.

Lowestoft ↗

Coverage of the Wherry Lines would be incomplete without a brief foray into the Suffolk terminus. Although its glory days receiving trainloads of holidaymakers are long past, the station's proximity to the pedestrianised town centre and the South Beach remain an advantage. To the right of the station can be seen the remains of the track which led across the main road to the fish-wharves, the source of another long lost traffic.

Acle ↑

The construction of the village bypass cut off the original station approach road, the remains of which are hidden in the trees beyond the passing coach. Out of view to the left, the present road access is from the new Reedham Road seen in the foreground. All the station buildings date from 1883, the year that the line was opened, and all remain externally much as built.

Acle Straight ↗

The current method for replacing life-expired track is to replace the train service with buses and to flood the track with machines to do the work. One of the stages in such an operation is shown here between Acle and Yarmouth with traffic on the parallel A47 Acle Straight passing in the background.

Acle Straight ↗

A little nearer to Stracey Arms, another part of the work involves specialist lifting devices loading the worn out track onto a train of flat wagons for conveyance from the site to a suitable point for disposal.

Yarmouth Vauxhall ↘

The terminus is still in the same location as it has been since 1844, despite being engulfed by the Asda supermarket and its approach roads. This arrangement has, however, allowed the railway authorities to abandon the former approach road bridge, seen in the background, over the River Bure.

Lost lines of South Norfolk.

Much of the railway system in what we have defined under this heading has been
closed for many years. But many traces can still be found, as shown in this selection of photographs.

Gorleston ↑

The s-bend line of the railway through the town can be seen to good effect. While the section from Links Road in the south, and under Bridge Road towards the site of the former station, passes through a residential area, the route of the closed railway beyond that point proved convenient when the A12 trunk road was improved to bypass the town and head towards Yarmouth. The new outer harbour is taking shape to the north of the river mouth.

Hopton ⬇

Bounded by the sea and the A12 to east and west respectively, it is clear that around half of the village is given over to holiday accommodation. The former railway bisected the community from the bottom right-hand corner in an almost straight line over the county boundary towards Corton and the northern outskirts of Lowestoft.

Haddiscoe ↖

Heading north, the East Suffolk Line re-crossed the River Waveney from Norfolk into Suffolk via St.Olaves Swing Bridge which, like that at Beccles, had been reconstructed on a new alignment in the 1920s. The bridge piers remain on each side of the river to this day, as does the associated signal box, now in private ownership.

Haddiscoe ⬇

Looking in the opposite direction, the route taken across Haddiscoe Marshes is unmistakeable. The imprint of the piers of the original bridge can be seen in the reeds to the right of the later remains. The present Norwich to Lowestoft line passes from right to left with Haddiscoe station visible on the right.

Beccles ↗

To the north-east of the town, we look from Suffolk into Norfolk as the route of the former East Suffolk Line heads across the River Waveney and then curves to the left, towards Aldeby and Haddiscoe; this section closed almost fifty years ago. The piers of 1920s swing bridge remain as does an indication of the alignment of its predecessor slightly to the left.

Beccles ↘

Local anglers make good use of the abandoned structure to pursue their chosen form of relaxation.

Left:
Beccles ➜
The River Waveney flows round the west of the town, marking the boundary between Norfolk and Suffolk. While the course of the Waveney Valley line from Tivetshall is obvious on the Norfolk side, its route through the town is less so, the only clue being the slightly angled alignment of two of the industrial units built on the formation as the line curved round to the junction, out of view at the top right hand corner.

Right:
Geldeston ⬉
The unusual feature of this location is the survival of the enormous goods shed, virtually unaltered. It provides a stark contrast with the station buildings of similar age which now form an immaculate twenty-first century residence.

Geldeston ←

Further west, between Harleston and Ditchingham, the railway formation has been used to improve the A143 road, but, east of the latter village, the line is "off the beaten track", among the water meadows. The station can be seen in the middle distance above the northern end of Geldeston Dyke, while the village is on the right. The road towards Ellingham winds its way to the top of the view.

Ellingham ⬈

Spot the original station building! The chimneys are the obvious clue, but, with alterations and additions to left and right, it has been fairly well disguised. The platform wall survives at each end of the site and has been used to good advantage as a feature of the property.

Harleston ↑

One of the most impressive former railway buildings, but slightly different in that it is still used for commercial purposes, this is a fine example of the art of restoration. Even the chimneys bear a striking similarity to those shown in 100 year-old photographs, although it seems unlikely that they serve their original purpose.

Starston ↗

This station closed in 1866, barely a decade after it opened, and, as such, is one of the most remarkable survivors on the line.

Pulham Market ⬇

In view of the relatively small communities that they served, stations on the Waveney Valley line were, with very few exceptions, built to rather generous proportions. As we have already seen, many of them have survived to become substantial residential properties some 150 years after they were constructed. What is seen here is typical of the way both buildings and land have been used to maximum effect by the present owner.

Ashwellthorpe ⬇

The station dates from 1881 and the remaining buildings, though extended and modernised, are typical of the architecture of the time. One platform remains and the approach road follows much the same alignment as it has for well over a century.

Ashwellthorpe ↖

To many motorists heading north on the B1113 towards Norwich, the remains of a railway station here is probably something of a mystery. It was the only station on the line linking Forncett with Wymondham and closed one week after the outbreak of World War II. The busy collection of light industrial units is prominent. Wymondham can be seen right at the top of the photo.

From Wymondham to Wells – the spine of Norfolk.

Opened in stages between 1846 and 1857, this line closed in equally piecemeal fashion between 1964 and 1989.
Although sections of the route have been obliterated entirely, the remainder has developed a surprisingly wide variety of uses.

Kimberley Park ↖

The southernmost stretch of the line, between Wymondham and Dereham, is now the Mid Norfolk Railway. It is normally diesel operated, but steam trains have run each summer from 2006 to 2008. One such train holds up traffic on the Norwich to Watton main road as it runs into the station, whose buildings have changed little since British Railways withdrew the passenger services in October 1969.

Hardingham ↟
This station, a few miles further north, has been restored but is not a stopping point for Mid Norfolk Railway trains. As in the previous picture, the engine is Great Western Railway designed 0-6-0PT no 9466, which was built in 1952, and was making its third visit to the railway.

Dereham ↑
This is the headquarters of the preserved line, and here we see the southern approaches to the station. A new road and the white-roofed Sports Centre building have obliterated all traces of the triangular junction leading to the line that ran westwards to Kings Lynn until 1968.

Dereham ↗

The modern structures on the former railway land contrast with the older buildings which provide reminders of rural industries to the east of the line.

Dereham ↖

We drop down for a closer look at the station, which underwent major restoration work in the early 21st century. Illustrating the wide variety of diesel power to be found here, there are six locomotives on show, of six different classes.

North Elmham ✔

The Mid Norfolk Railway has plans to extend northwards from Dereham as far as County School and in 2009 the tracks were still in place as far as North Elmham. Here the red brick station buildings stand next to the B1145 crossing, whilst the adjacent complex of white buildings was once a milk depot. In bygone days, this despatched a train carrying milk to London, which ran seven days a week.

County School ↖

The next station northwards took its name not from a local parish, but from the nearby educational establishment which became Watts Naval School and prepared young men for a seafaring career. The station was restored as part of a short-lived preservation venture during the 1990s, but later settled to life as a tearoom and picnic area.

County School ↗

Here the tracks are still in place, and may one day be extended southwards again, to join up with the Mid Norfolk Railway at North Elmham. The station was at one time the junction for a branch line to Wroxham, which bore off eastwards at Broom Green, a mile or so to the north.

Foulsham ↗

Before continuing northwards, we will make a short detour to Foulsham, the first station on the line to Wroxham. As at so many places, the station, seen at the bottom of this view, was some way from the centre of the village. The building is substantially intact, with only a few modifications since passenger trains were withdrawn in 1952. All other stations on this line were built to the same design.

Ryburgh ⬉

Returning to the Wells line, the path of the railway runs from the centre bottom of our picture to a point where it meets the main road through the village. The station site is now an access road to the maltings, and the industrial complex has extended over the course of the line, with gigantic silos standing where the trains once ran.

Fakenham ⬉

The site of the station has been obliterated by housing, but one surviving feature of the railway in the town is this bridge, which once carried the road over the line just north of the station. Now it spans just a tree choked cutting, and the encroaching greenery hides the fact that this is a substantial three-arched structure.

Fakenham ←
Heading northwards out of the town, the course of the railway becomes clearer once more. At this former level crossing, the little brick hut and gatekeepers' cottage provide tangible reminders of the past.

Walsingham ↗

Redundant railway stations have, as we have seen, been converted to a variety of uses. The fate of Walsingham station has to be one of the most unusual, for it now forms the Russian Orthodox Chapel of Saint Seraphim. While the building has been extended, and has gained a distinctive bell tower, the platform remains, facing onto a coach park where the lines were. To the left of the coaches, the brick built goods shed is a further reminder of days gone by.

Walsingham ↑

Approaching Walsingham, the clearly defined path of the railway passes the Slipper Chapel complex before continuing across the open countryside to the town itself. The Chapel is an important religious centre, and although there was never a station here, the railway ran pilgrimage specials to this spot. As there was no platform, the passengers had to clamber down from the carriages to ground level, a practice which would no doubt be strictly forbidden today. From here the pilgrims would walk the rest of the way to the shrines at Walsingham.

Walsingham 🡿
Many of the features of the historic and compact little town can be seen in this picture. Continuing with our railway theme though, the old line still marks the western extremity of the town, where the goods shed is the last building before we reach the fields at the top of the picture.

Wells ✎

Following the route of the standard gauge line between the two towns, the Wells and Walsingham Railway started running in 1979, and this 10¼-inch gauge tourist line is popular with summer visitors to the area. This is the northern terminus, next to the main coast road, with the locomotive "Norfolk Hero" waiting to set out on its 30 minute journey. The signalbox was moved here from Swainsthorpe, where it once controlled the passage of express trains on the Liverpool Street to Norwich line.

Wells ↖

The line from Fakenham enters at bottom right, and passes a row of parked mobile homes before coming to the former station area, almost exactly in the centre of our picture and now occupied by various industrial units. Following a semicircular course from the station site, the branch line to the harbour is easy to follow round to the quayside. We can also follow the line from Heacham, entering the picture at top left, as it curves round to the south of the town to the point where it was bridged by the coast road. North of the road however, there is no trace of its continuing curved approach to the terminus.

North & West Norfolk – empty trackbeds and electric trains.

This section takes us from Holkham, just west of Wells, in an anticlockwise direction around the north-west corner of the county to Kings Lynn along closed lines. We then head south on the electrified route towards the Cambridgeshire border, before returning to Kings Lynn to cover the Dereham branch, part open but most closed, to a point a few miles east of Swaffham.

Holkham ←

This is the point where the West Norfolk line came closest to the sea. The coast road winds its way past the lake and wooded area at the northern end of the Holkham estate while the railway took a somewhat more direct route across the marshes. Lady Ann's Drive cuts across the railway formation heading north from the estate village towards the beach.

Burnham Market ↖

The station stood next to a level crossing on the road to Fakenham. Over fifty years after closure, it is still recognisable, despite being somewhat hemmed in by later developments. The retention of the platform wall and the addition of a railway van on the old trackbed help in its identification.

Burnham Market ↙

The route describes a smooth curve as it heads south-west, providing an effective boundary between residential properties and the wide open spaces devoted to agriculture. The parish church adds to the traditional feel of a typically genteel village.

Sedgeford ↖

Little appears to have altered since the last train passed through at the end of 1964, with the signal box, imported from Stow, but carrying a spurious "Sedgeford" nameboard. Even the level crossing gateposts are still fulfilling their intended purpose.

Heacham ↓
The West Norfolk line enters from the left and curves through 90° to join the line of route to Kings Lynn which threads its way between the ranks of caravans towards the top of the picture. The line from Hunstanton appears from the bottom right corner. The Wash coastline puts in a token appearance top right.

Hunstanton ↙
A view from 1956 helps to illustrate the changes which have taken place here. At this time, Summer Sundays saw around ten trains arrive in a two hour period before lunch, disgorging several thousand day trippers. The sidings opposite the gasworks would be full of coaches which were not required to return home until after tea.

Hunstanton ↙
It is obvious when compared with the previous view that the demands of the holidaymakers were rather simpler half a century earlier. Not only does car parking space dominate the former station site, but the number of undercover attractions has increased dramatically, as has the amount of holiday accommodation, suggesting stays of more than just one day.

Heacham →

Apart from the presence of a railway coach, there is little to suggest from this angle that this is a former station. However, closer inspection reveals the survival of the Hunstanton bound waiting room, complete with awning, towards the lower left corner. The "West Norfolk" public house across the road also gives a clue in that the branch across to Wells was promoted under that title.

Snettisham ↑

What was the goods yard is now littered with all manner of scrap debris, with the unmistakeable shape of the goods shed surrounded by vehicles awaiting what may be their ultimate fate. By contrast, the former station buildings, its curving approach road and the neighbouring properties have a neat and well kept appearance.

Dersingham 🖝
Here the site has been adapted with minimum alterations. The trackbed between the platforms has been used as an access road to the yard, retaining the original station approach as the parking area for residential use. Careful scrutiny among the myriad collection of construction materials, reveals several surviving railway buildings, the most noteworthy, in addition to the house itself, being the signal box.

Wolferton ↖

With a high proportion of the buildings provided for Royal use, this is clearly no ordinary country station, although it offered the same public facilities as any other. Even the signal box and the cottages provided for railway employees had a superior finish. The ornate building in the foreground is named as the post office on a 1905 Ordnance Survey plan.

North Wootton 🖎
The track here ran at right-angles to the road which crosses the view from left to right. With little else but marshes to the west, it made sense to build the gabled house and main station premises on the Kings Lynn bound platform, with the two smaller brick buildings on that which took passengers to Hunstanton. Much of the goods yard site is taken up by the long, low unit to the left.

Hunstanton Line ↑

Hunstanton is in the far distance and the line heads towards Kings Lynn via Wolferton. It then skirts the west end of North Wootton village before crossing Edward Benefer Way and heading through the northern suburbs of the town. The final sharp curve brings it towards Kings Lynn Junction at the bottom of the picture. The line towards Middleton is the right hand of the two lines at the bottom of the view.

Kings Lynn ↖

The main line from Ely passes two supermarkets, occupying the site of the former goods yard, as it makes its way into the terminus. The disused Docks Branch shows as a near perfect S-bend on the right; the remains of this line are used for reversal of sand trains to and from Middleton, located about 3 miles to the east on the former line to Swaffham.

Kings Lynn ↘
The terminus presents a neat and compact appearance with easy access to car parks on both sides. Apart from the fact that the present brickwork is almost clinically clean, the station frontage has altered surprisingly little down the years. The platforms retain an impressive length of protective awnings.

Kings Lynn ↑
The line towards Ely cuts a straight path diagonally across the top right hand corner of this view, passing under Hardwick Road. At the bottom is the Southern Bypass with the River Nar meandering its way from bottom right to top left past the recently cleared site of the old "Muck Works".

Kings Lynn ↖

A slightly different view of the same area helps to link the closed M&GN line covered in an earlier section with the line to Ely. Harbour Junction was located directly under the by-pass bridge at bottom centre while the trackbed of the old Harbour Branch is obvious as it makes a bee-line for the quays top right.

Watlington ↖

Much changed here in the run-up to Electrification in 1992. Kings Lynn bound trains use the lengthened platform on the left, while those heading south call at a completely new platform north of the level crossing. The tall signal box which now controls the barriers retains its earlier name of Magdalen Road and has a commanding view of approaching traffic on both road and rail.

Watlington ↘

This view from the opposite side gives a clear impression of the platform formerly used in the Ely direction, together with the restored station buildings now in residential use.

Downham ↖

As the car parking facilities suggest, this station has become something of a commuter location, being less than 30 minutes from Cambridge and under 1½ hours from Kings Cross. The carstone station buildings and other facilities have been carefully restored, giving the place a neat and businesslike appearance.

Middleton ↘

Returning to the line which we saw branching off earlier at Kings Lynn Junction, the extensive workings that have provided a source of freight traffic for many years are shown here to the north of the Swaffham line, closed in 1968. The former, rather picturesque, station features in the bottom right-hand corner.

Above:

Dunham ↙

The road in the foreground is still carried over the formation by a three-arch bridge, complete with typical parapet walls. Three adapted, substantial station buildings stand in a diagonal line. The first, with the caravan adjacent, is the former goods shed; to its right is the main station with its distinctive gable end and chimneys, while the third, on the opposite platform, backs onto the field.

Left:

Swaffham →

Forty years after it closed, the route of the railway to Dereham remains obvious, curving from bottom centre of the picture to the top left-hand corner, with the former branch line to Watton forking off through a line of trees to top centre. The station site was adjacent to the Fakenham road, left of centre, with the market square and parish church to the right. On the extreme left the A47 bypass, en route towards Norwich, sweeps past the dominating wind turbine.

Fransham ↖

Perhaps it's just the angle or maybe the buildings themselves but this looks more like a model than the real thing. However, it is actually the site of the station with the main building in the bottom right-hand corner and the platform almost completely intact. The owner clearly has more than a passing interest in railways.

Near Fransham ↗

The excavating machine at work towards the bottom left-hand corner of this view is in the process of removing what remains of the railway embankment. Similar action has already taken place to the right, beyond the road.

The Breckland line – reminders of the past on a busy cross country route.

The line between Norwich and Ely dates back to 1845, and at one time formed part of the principal route between Norwich and London. In 2009 there was an hourly service for most of the day between Norwich and Cambridge, and a similar frequency of trains to the Midlands and North. During the early 21st century, the line has hosted a number of special trains, hauled by preserved main line steam locomotives, and we shall look at some of these in the next section.

Thetford ⬆

A steam hauled special train passes the station on its way to Yarmouth in May 2001, hauled by class 5 4-6-0 no.45407. The early flint built station building is still standing, next to a later brick-built addition, dating back to 1889. Local flints were also used in the construction of the Railway Tavern, which stands next to the bend in the road, still performing its original function.

Harling Road ↗

Another of the steam hauled specials passes the station, heading for Norwich in May 2008. Locomotive no. 60019 "Bittern" is one of the A4 class built in the 1930s to haul express trains on the East Coast main line. The original station building and railway cottages, dating back to the opening of the route, can be seen beyond the front coach of the train, contrasting with more recent housing development.

Eccles Road ↑

Early in 2009 the line retained much of its traditional character, with manual signalboxes, small wayside stations, and, in places, the old fashioned telegraph poles and wires. All these features can be seen in this view of the station. Its train service is sparse, with only two weekday trains in each direction booked to stop there in the 2009 timetable.

Eccles Road ↘

A private siding was built as late as 1985 to serve the nearby distribution and warehousing centre of Richard Johnston Ltd. We can follow its sharply curved course from the main line, running across the top of the picture, to the warehouses. Originally built to handle grain traffic, which ceased after a few years, it has seen occasional use in the 21st century for loads as diverse as aggregates and seed potatoes.

Attleborough ↑
Many of the old buildings remain, although the site of the former goods yard is now occupied by a meticulously maintained bowls green. To the right of the picture, the goods shed survives in private ownership.

Left:

Spooner Row →

As at Eccles Road, this little station exhibits traditional signalling and telegraph posts. Here the 2009 train service is even more basic, with two trains to Norwich and one in the return direction timetabled to stop – but only by request. The station cottages still stand behind the platform, opposite the signal box.

Below:

Spooner Row ↑

A class 158 diesel unit runs over the level crossing as it passes the station with a train from Norwich to Chesterfield in November 2008.

Wymondham ←

Another of the famous class A4 Pacifics, no. 60009 "Union of South Africa" visited the line on its way to Norwich in October 2003, and a large crowd congregated on the platforms and footbridge to watch it go by.

Wymondham ↑

Snow in 2003 was almost as rare an event as the visit of a steam locomotive. A train for Cambridge stops at a rather chilly Wymondham in the January of that year.

Spinks Lane ↖

A gang of workmen is busy next to the level crossing, just east of Wymondham, as a train from the Midlands passes on the last stage of its long cross-country journey to Norwich. The open area to the right of the picture, immediately behind the train, is the site of the short-lived Spinks Lane station, which lasted for less than a year after the line opened.

Hethersett ↑
Sidings were laid to serve an Air Ministry fuel depot here in 1943, and these were very busy during the war years. Perhaps surprisingly, the sidings were still in place within the depot in 2008, although disconnected from the main line. The buildings of Hethersett station, closed in 1966, are to the left of the siding, while the dual carriageway A11 is prominent on the other side of the railway. A planning application for a travellers' site was submitted in late 2008 presaging a change of use for this reminder of Norfolk's military aviation heritage.

South west of Norwich ⬉
Another steam hauled special ran to Norwich from London Kings Cross in August 2008, and is seen here passing under the Norwich Southern bypass. This time the engine was 4-6-2 no. 6233 "Duchess of Sutherland", one of a class built for the London Midland & Scottish Railway back in the 1930s. Although it spent most of its working life on express trains between Euston and Glasgow, it does have a Norfolk connection, having been an exhibit at Bressingham Steam Museum for some 25 years from 1971 before being overhauled for main line use.

South west of Norwich ↗

Eaton village is in the middle distance of this view stretching across to the distant city, where the City Hall and Cathedral are prominent. In the foreground, no. 60019 is nearing its destination with the special train from London in May 2008.

Keswick ↑
The same train was photographed again shortly afterwards, crossing the River Yare with Keswick Mill in the foreground.

Lakenham ⬋

The viaduct carries the electrified main line to Ipswich and Liverpool Street over the Breckland Line and the River Yare. We have caught up with "Bittern" again, a feat that would be impossible to achieve by road.

Lakenham ⬅

The railway is now keeping company with the River Tas as "Duchess of Sutherland" passes under the Stoke Holy Cross Road. In the early days there was a level crossing here. It was soon replaced by a bridge, but the little flint built crossing keeper's cottage is still there, visible above the locomotive.

Trowse ↖

This bridge over the River Wensum was brought into use in 1987, and is unusual in being a swing bridge carrying an overhead electrified railway. It is the third bridge to span the river at this point, and the centre pivot of its predecessor is still there, with a particularly hardy tree growing from it. With part of Laurence & Scott's works to the left, another steam hauled special train heads for Norwich.

Norwich ↗

The depot at Crown Point is responsible for the maintenance of the trains used on the London trains and local services around Norwich. It occupies a cramped site between the lines from Trowse and those to the coast, and the curvature of the tracks is particularly noticeable from this viewpoint.

Below:

Norwich ↖

Here we have another look at Crown Point depot, with the coastal lines coming in on the right. Norwich station is in the centre of the picture with the Riverside shopping and entertainment complex to the left. A generation hence, people will find it difficult to believe that this area was once occupied by railway yards and heavy industry.

Norwich ⬊

The familiar frontage of the city's station is seen from an entirely novel angle. To the right of the station, Koblenz Avenue occupies an area which was crisscrossed with railway tracks until the 1990s.

The Bittern Line – a rural ride to the seaside.

Since 1997, the line between Norwich and the coast at Cromer and Sheringham has been marketed as the Bittern Line. Once threatened with closure, passenger usage has increased in recent years. In this section, we shall also look at the long-closed secondary route from North Walsham to Cromer, via Mundesley.

Whitlingham Junction ↗

Here the Bittern line parts company with the Wherry lines and heads northwards, passing between the Dussindale development and St Andrew's Business Park. Moving into open country, it skirts Thorpe End, Rackheath and Salhouse, before reaching Wroxham, where the Broad is prominent to the right of the picture.

Wroxham ⬇

A diesel unit bound for Norwich crosses the Bure just south of the station. Although the town is an important Broads centre, this glimpse of the boatyard buildings is the only view that passengers get of the waterways.

Wroxham ↗

A minute or so earlier, the same train was photographed arriving at the platform. In its heyday the station was the junction for a branch line to County School, the route of which is now occupied by the Bure Valley Railway as far as Aylsham.

North of Wroxham ↗

A train of tankers carrying condensate – a waste product of the North Sea gas industry – rumbles through the countryside near Sloley. The material is brought by pipeline from Bacton Gas Terminal to North Walsham, where it is loaded on to rail and taken to Harwich for treatment. In 2009, this was one of the few regular freight trains to run in Norfolk.

Worstead ↑

Only a single track runs through the unstaffed station these days, but the former northbound platform remains. The old signalbox, now in private ownership, is at the top of the picture, partly shielded by trees, while the house provided for the station master is prominent to the left.

North Walsham ↓

A busy moment at North Walsham. At the bottom of the picture, a diesel unit leaves for Sheringham, while a similar train stands in the platform, bound for Norwich. The wagons of the condensate train are in the yard to the east of the station, and a locomotive waits by the siding entrance, ready to take another loaded train to Harwich. The main road on the left of the picture has been built on the course of the M&GN line, and the town's other station stood roughly where the coach and lorries are waiting at the traffic lights.

North Walsham →

The engine for the condensate train stands by the gate giving access to the sidings.

Paston & Knapton ↖

The intermediate station between North Walsham and Mundesley was named after the neighbouring villages of Paston and Knapton. It was closer to the latter, which can be seen to the top of the picture. From this angle, the course of the footpath which once connected the village to the station can clearly be seen across the field in the centre. Rail traffic ceased in 1964, but the building is now a private residence and has changed little in over a century.

130

Mundesley ⬋

The housing development in the top left hand corner occupies the land on which the town's four-platformed station once stood. However, a line of trees clearly indicates the course of the railway as it turns westwards towards Overstrand and Cromer. To the left is a terrace of former railway cottages, their timbered gables mirroring those at Paston.

Mundesley

Here the same trees provide a link with the previous picture. By contrast with the winding course of the coast road, the railway cutting heads straight across the countryside to a point due south of the "golf ball" that is Trimingham Radar Station. For some distance beyond here, there is no trace of the line, which has been ploughed over in the years since the last train ran between Mundesley and Cromer at Easter 1953.

Overstrand ⬈

Here too, the station has been converted into a private house, sympathetically extended to maintain the atmosphere of the railway building. A notable feature is the roof of the subway, which once provided public access to the platforms. From here the line continued westwards to join the Bittern Line at a junction close to what is now Roughton Road station.

Gunton ↙

Returning to the Bittern Line, we come to Gunton station where all trains now use the old southbound platform. On the other platform, the former station building is in private use and has been restored with a railway theme – the engine and trucks to the top of the picture are purely decorative. Present day passengers have only a couple of bus shelters to protect them from the elements.

Cromer ⬎

The town has a complex railway history, being served by the Great Eastern Railway from Norwich and the M&GN from Melton Constable, each line having its own station. Since 1954, trains have used the centrally-sited M&GN station (Cromer Beach) and the GER station, the aptly named Cromer High, at the top of the hill on the outskirts of the town, has been abandoned. The site of the latter station is in the foreground, partly covered by a housing development and partly still derelict land. At the top of the picture we can see the curving route of the Bittern Line.

Cromer ⬆
Autumn leaves make for a colourful scene, as a Bittern Line train crosses the bridge carrying the railway over the Felbrigg to Cromer road. The line is now in open countryside again, as it loops round to run into the town from the west.

Cromer ↗

A steam locomotive returned to the line for the first time in some 45 years when class B1 4-6-0 no. 61264 worked three special trains to and from Norwich in April 2006. With the town of Cromer and the North Sea in the distance, the engine steams through the countryside on its way back to Norwich.

Cromer ↖

All trains to and from Sheringham have to reverse here, as the station is a terminus. The fine old station building is still externally intact, but the railway itself is very much hemmed in by a supermarket which has been built on the land formerly occupied by the goods yard and locomotive shed.

Right:

East Runton ↗

The two lines meet a mile or so from Cromer station, and here we see the line from Sheringham running diagonally across the picture to meet the line from Norwich, which curves in sharply from the right. Until the early 1960s, a third line, built to avoid the reversal at Cromer station, created a triangle of tracks here. Its course is easy to trace from the air, running over the viaduct on the left and through the trees to connect with the Norwich line at the bottom right hand corner of the picture. The area bounded by the three lines is now a caravan park.

Left:

West Runton ↗

We catch up with no. 61264 and the 2006 steam train again, this time passing West Runton village as it heads for Sheringham. The engine is an appropriate choice, as this type was a familiar sight on the line during the 1950s.

138

Sheringham ↑

Now we come to the terminus of the Bittern Line, where, since 1967, Norwich trains have used a basic platform to the east of the road, whilst the original station has become the headquarters of the North Norfolk Railway. The length of track between the two stations has been removed, and the extremities of the two railways face each other, only a short distance apart across the road. Since this photograph was taken the parties involved have agreed to install a level crossing and to reinstate the connection between the two stations.

The North Norfolk Railway – steam engines by the sea.

Running for just over five miles between Holt and Sheringham, the North Norfolk Railway has been operating since 1975, and, with a largely steam-worked service, is now a major attraction for visitors to the area. The line was formerly part of the M&GN branch between Melton Constable and Cromer.

Holt ↖

The terminus here is located in a wooded area to the north of the town. At bottom left of the picture, the station building is partially shaded by the trees. It was originally located at Stalham and was rebuilt here in 2001/2. In the centre is the museum building, which is based on the goods shed which once stood at Thursford. A Routemaster bus, far from the streets of its native London, provides a connection into the town centre during the high season, and next to this is the miniature railway which provides a further diversion for summer visitors.

Holt ⬀

Just north of the station are Bridge Road Carriage sheds. These were constructed in 2006/7 with the aid of a grant from the Heritage Lottery Fund to provide covered accommodation for the railway's historic coaches, which had previously been at the mercy of the harsh North Norfolk winters. By April 2007, the buildings were externally complete. The surrounding trees ensure that the sheds are hidden from the nearby road and do not detract from the surrounding countryside.

Weybourne ⬅

On the last day of 2005 a train passes the sheds and yard as it approaches Weybourne station. The rays of the setting sun illuminate the locomotives, "Martello", a visitor from Bressingham Museum, and class J15 0-6-0 no 65462, which is one of the fleet of engines based on the line.

Near Weybourne ↗
For most of the journey between Weybourne and Sheringham the line is in sight of the sea. Visiting V2 2-6-2 no. 60800 "Green Arrow" steams through the deserted countryside on a bright Boxing Day 2004 – the kind of day that is guaranteed to blow away the Christmas cobwebs! The engine was on loan from the National Railway Museum at York.

Sheringham ↗

On another perfect winter's afternoon a train throws its shadow across the golf course as it heads westwards away from Sheringham. Groups of golfers pause from their game to watch it go by.

Sheringham ↑
A few seconds later the long shadows are even more pronounced as class N7 0-6-2T no. 69621 continues on its way towards Weybourne and Holt. Snow is still lying in the southern lips of the bunkers, where the rays of the low winter sun have been unable to reach.